Uncovering the Veil

FORGIVENESS IS THE KEY TO RELEASE ALL STRONG HOLDS

SIMPLY BLESSED

UNCOVERING THE VEIL
FORGIVENESS IS THE KEY TO RELEASE ALL STRONG HOLDS

Scripture quotations from the Holy Bible, King James Version (Authorized Version). First published in 1611. Quoted from the KJV Classic Reference Bible.

iUniverse books may be ordered through booksellers or by contacting:

iUniverse
1663 Liberty Drive
Bloomington, IN 47403
www.iuniverse.com
1-800-Authors (1-800-288-4677)

ISBN: 978-1-5320-4733-6 (sc)
ISBN: 978-1-5320-4734-3 (e)

Library of Congress Control Number: 2018904466

Print information available on the last page.

iUniverse rev. date: 04/13/2018

Introduction

The purpose of this book is to let everyone understand that you are not alone. I am going to take you through my journey where my faith was tested, I was totally disconnected from GOD and how I was lost, vulnerable and naïve. I was looking for answers and guidance from someone to help me and how GOD always manage to put people in my path to protect me.

This book will help guide you and bring your self-esteem and confidence back. If you every had any doubt where you were unable to do accomplish anything, and you are confused and need better understanding, Welcome to a new beginning where your eyes will be opened your faith will be strengthened. This Guide is to help you heal and restore what has been stolen from you. It will guide you to make better life choices and no longer leave yourself in a box. WELCOME TO YOUR NEW BEGINNING.

Author's Note

Follow me into my journey and let me guide you into my life which brought about this book to its birth. I came from a broken home where I felt alone. A cry for help was nonexistent and I had been neglected by my hard-working mother who lived for us but forgot to nurture us. I had a father who could not keep his dick in his pants because he was lusting after other women while my mother struggled to take care of us. Both parents were young and very naïve. I had family who saw me daily and still didn't know I even existed. I was molested at six years old by a family member on my father's side, my uncle whom I thought loved me but hurt me because I was his favorite niece. I was visiting my dad and spent the night at his house, he brought me home a couple of days later. When I returned home I fainted. all I remember is my mother going to hospital to find out what was wrong with me. I was in the hospital for a very long time in a coma, paralyzed and blind physically but I saw everything going on. The Doctor could not tell her what was wrong and why I was in the hospital for more than half of the school year. My father side of the family said that my father's current wife put roots on me. I was molested and rapped by my mother's boyfriend when I was eight. I ate myself into an eating disorder. I was already a thick young lady, and I looked older then what I was. I was a target for older guys at the age of thirteen! Males looked at me differently. I was a big girl with curves in all the right places, thick legs, and long hair, and a pretty face. My mom put me and my brother in a program called THE BOYS AND GIRLS OF AMERICA where I had a crush on this young man whom I liked very much. I and some of my friends hung together and I ended up getting sexually assaulted by my crush's best friend at the time whom my crush turns out to be my baby's father oh I didn't tell you I got pregnant at the tender age of fourteen. By the time I got in High School, a few, so called friends introduced me to the streets. I was unknown and out of my element and naive. I am talking drugs and liquor. Then my mother got married to an asshole who turned out to be a Coke-head. As years went by after few assholes along the way, all my female friends decided to become lesbians. I met this guy whom I thought was going to be a one-night stand turned into an eleven-year imprisonment on the out-side of the jail. Now I am an adult and I have four beautiful children. Now let me explain how the LORD has tested me time and time again. I was rapped, molested, beaten, had women and men gang members in my home, never had a stable place to stay, been working since the summer youth program and used the system as well just to try to stay afloat. I could not use it anymore. I was sick all the time I had no one to turn to and the LORD protected me from losing my sanity and made me a stronger woman today. I finished high school, went to college, and became a medical assistant. I been married and divorced. I am not a millionaire, but I sure feel like one because I have a dream and goals and my journey is not over whomever pick up this book let me guide you in your blessings, so you will be able to reach your inner self and smile through your adversity and know you are not alone.

AGE 5-6

At the age of 5 we (mom and dad) were living with my fraternal grandmother in a NEWARK project. It was very late one summer night I was around the age of 5, I spending the night with my grandmother when my uncle came in and started fondling me. I had no clue what was going on and to this day I still draw a blank trying to recall some of the details. It was too much for my little innocent mind to handle. He eventually left the room, and I went into the kitchen with my grandmother and that's when things started to change for me.

Shortly after that, without anyone knowing what happened to me, my family moved out of my fraternal grandmother's apartment into my maternal grandmother's home. At this time, I was just in the kindergarten and for some reason still unknown to any including the doctors, I ended up in the hospital and could not see or move and was in a coma with no explanation to-date. Nothing else was ever done or said about it.

AGE 8

At the age of 8 my mother was dating this man. My mom had ended their relationship, however, no one at home knew about it. One day he came by and my mother was not at home. Only me and my younger brother were at home in our apartment, which was part of my grandmother's house and how he was able to gain access to our apartment. Everyone else was downstairs when he came into my room and said to me "you're going to do what your mother won't". He then raped me while my younger brother was in the bed with me asleep! I then went downstairs to tell my family and I didn't know then but in that short time I lost my voice and was unable to tell anyone about what happened to me. As time went on I began to struggle in school both mentally and physically. I went through different kinds of stages from urinating on myself to anxiety. I was teased and bullied in school as well. My school work suffered tremendously the traumatic events started taking a toll on me.

AGE 12

I went to the supermarket with my aunt and great aunt and opened a pack of cupcakes and ate it. On the way out of the store the police stopped us and took us to the office to show us me opening a pack of cupcakes. That's when my great aunt said, **"you're going to church with me".** I was baptized April 12, 1990.

My mother had been working all the time and decided to leave me and my brother with another great aunt during the day. We went to school in her district. I had a very difficult time with this great aunt, she treated us extremely unfairly, which contributed to additional negativity in school for me. I ended up living at my maternal grandmother's home again, buy this time she had passed. That's when me and my brother began going to the BOYS AND GIRLS CLUB. While going to the BGS I had a crush on a young man who is now my eldest daughter's father. While going to the BGC I met some friends and we went to one of the young men's home. I was left in the room with one of the boys and suddenly he began molesting me. We went then went back to the BGC and I waited for my mom come pick me up, I as usual never told her what had happened to me.

AGE 14-16

When I went back to the BGC I where I my daughter's father every now and then he would come by and see me at my home. One day he came over to visit during school hours and my maternal uncle came home from work for lunch and caught us. My boyfriend was so scared he jumped out the third-floor window and down the tree that stood in front of the house. A few months later I discovered I was pregnant.

By the time my mom and I discovered I was pregnant, it was already too late for an abortion. I had no clue about birth control or anything of that nature. My mom took me to the Surgical Center the only one that would do abortions for far along in the pregnancy, it was even too late for them to legally perform the abortion.

AGE 17-21

At the age of 17 I was visiting a friend and at that time my oldest daughter was 2, I hadn't been in a relationship with anyone at the time and found myself in a weird place in my life. I was just looking for a friend, just someone to spend time with. I was sitting on the stoop with my girlfriend. We were all talking and drinking, and this young man was talking to his friend and said "come here, I have someone I want you to meet. The young came over and was with another young lady, so he told the guy he will be right bac and he came back by himself. We started talking and I found myself not really interested, but he was cool though, so I went back a few times to see him and we had sex. I didn't want a relationship. I stopped talking to him for months. One day he called me and said, "you don't know how to call no body" I said to him "you were supposed to be a one-night stand". So, I gave him a chance.

As time went on in our relationship, he gave me his life story to find out that he wasn't the age he told me and the people he was residing with were not his real parents. He started crying, he was still in school and so was I. He decided he wanted to drop out of school, I felt even more sorry for him. I said to myself, I am ready to move on my out on own and was already helping my mom and her husband pay the bills. I decided to move with him and we became closer he ask me a question that I was not prepared for. He as me who do you love more me or GOD, I said him with me being young and naïve, not knowing the person had an ulterior motive and not understanding that I put man before GOD was the worst thing I could ever do.

My Life With Sammy

As time went on, I started to see things that I couldn't understand. This man took me through all kinds of hell and back. I found out the people he was living with were junkies and not his parents. Earlier in the relationship I felt even more compelled to try to make this relationship work so he can understand that I had his best interest at heart, well that still didn't turn out well. He smoked weed, I said ok that's not that bad I don't do it if he doesn't do it around me and my daughter. Now we are in our own place and I am going to school and to work while he was staying home. He made his money by selling drugs and working odd jobs, I don't know why I thought this was ok and he always had friends come over our house. One day my girlfriend called me unexpected and said can she stay for a little bit her mom kicked her out, I said of course. That was very stupid of me because l knew she was extremely promiscuous. I never thought she would do the unthinkable to me. I came home from work one day and she was in the bed with Sammie with just her panties on sleep under the covers like everything was all right. Talking about a broken heart and it didn't end there, I get a knock on the door by another young lady that evening she was about 7 months pregnant she was very distraught and angry asking me where was Sammie. I asked who are you she said his baby's mother. Talk about devastated, I was beyond devastated. I cannot believe this was happening. I cried for weeks, as time went on I said let's go to church, he agreed.

Remember the young lady I told you about earlier, the one that was with him when I first met him? The same young lady was going to the church we joined, and she kept talking mad crap. I had to leave the church because the air was super thick, I couldn't concentrate. she followed me out side and started physically attacking me. I ended up fighting after church. That made me even more angry, a week before I found out about the girl he impregnated as well as dropping out of school and then lost his job. Everything was on me, this was crazy and as time went on he finally introduced me to his mother and his father they lived in the projects. My daughter was about 4 years old and I had no kids with at the time. Why didn't I just leave. I met his mom to find out that wasn't his real mother it was his stepmother and his father was not to fond of American women and he spoke very little English. His dad was from the Dominican Republic. His stepmother at the time was given me great advice about Sammie, I should have listened I don't know why I didn't. She was telling how he was a trouble child, he and his sister grew up with no mother she had past and their father left them alone in the Dominican Republic for two weeks. He was 3 and his sister was about age 1 when they found him and his sister in the house alone, eventually they found them. They stayed with their Paternal grandmother, that as well made me feel even more sympathy for him. I never was truly in love with him but all the events that kept happening made me feel like he had no one to turn to. I said, I'll stay by your side. We ended up moving in with his stepmother. We lived in the basement apartment, at that time I thought I was pregnant and that was one of the most challenging times in my life, it was crazy. He was never home. He had a job at the bodega store around where I grow up. Everyone knew me he started hanging out with people my mother never allowed me to hang with and the worst part he was hanging with one of the older people whom was known to smoke more than just weed, the older lady let's just call her June. He was always at that house on 11 street in the middle of the block, he never came home until dawn the following morning. One day I had to go look for him, the people that lived there said that he was upstairs with June. I went upstairs he was gone I heard a whisper and all the talk, yet I still didn't get it. I was about 7 months pregnant at the time, in my feelings and just tired of chasing and helping him. I was in a situation I didn't know how to get out of. He became very abusive mentally, physically, emotionally, spiritually. His stepmother was getting tired of him and his father was getting tired of him. I'm pregnant, I have a 5-year-old daughter going on 6. I sent her back to my live with my mom. It has getting to the point that I had to decide. I was very unhappy and uncomfortable.

I just had my baby and I needed piece of mind, I moved to a new apartment. You would have thought it would have gotten better but it didn't this place was like the projects on a whole different level. It was two buildings facing each other and both places needed to be cleaned. As time went on I started a new job. I was 21 and my youngest had just turned 1 year old. Let me tell you I was in this dark place in my life, very unhappy my baby father Sammie was working and selling drugs. I came home, and he had a bunch of people in my house and they were gang members. I said, "what the heck is going on here" he replied, "he got off early and he invited a few friends by". I asked him was he in a gang he told me no. I was OK with it. He said was just trying to get a tattoo. I asked him where are the kids, he replied, oh they are at a babysitter's house, I asked him "who is babysitting" he replied "Bella, she lives in 15f". I never asked how he knew her, it never dawned on me that he could have been having an affair with this girl until someone from the building told me they seen him and her together. I asked him who was that he said he knew her for a minute, it's was one night I was in my living room and he tried to have intercourse while his penis was dripping and smelly and I didn't want to have sex with him at all. I asked him what was wrong with it, why was it like that. I stopped having sex with him, I didn't trust him. I met these people it was an older couple and they said to me that I needed to clean my house. I didn't know what they meant by that at the time. I had gang members living with me, my brother living with and his friends. We all were living in a 1-bedroom apartment and Sammie lost his job. I was the only one working and was tired and crying every day. They took over my house and it was one night it was pitched black and I was in my living room sleep I woke up but was half asleep and I saw words in Hebrew written in flames going across my wall. I was very scared, I shut my eyes, I couldn't believe it. The night before Sammie and his friends took my bible that I got when I was first baptized, and they ripped the pages out of my bible and smoked drugs with it, I was so hurt.

I got to the point where I was just lost and confused. I met this young lady who had an autistic daughter her name was Ne-ne, she was a former prostitute was running away from her current boyfriend and a situation she no longer could handle, he was an OG blood gang member.

We started going to church with the older couple previously mentioned, who are now my second daughter's godparents. They got me through a lot of hard times, with the word and Bible study. They were talking to me and explained why I needed to spiritually cleanse my home. At that time, in no way did I understand what CLEAN THE HOUSE meant. I told them I had already cleaned the house, but when he broke it down to me and said you need to spiritually cleanse your home.

It gotten so bad living in that place, they took over their house. The gang members were still having parties, they had written on all my walls with spray paint. I had to just go! I had to leave! I left and moved in with my mom in a studio apartment. Sammy didn't want to let me leave, he said you can leave, but I had to leave his daughter. Sammy had the woman he had babysitting keep her. I found out she was a schizophrenic manic. I had no choice, he would not let me get my daughter, that hurt so bad.

I had been staying with my mom for a few months and would missed Sammy. He had been trying to make amends and I end up pregnant by him again. I didn't want to keep the baby, I went to go pick up my second daughter from the babysitter's house and ended up in a bus accident on my way to the house. I wasn't ready to have another child and had an abortion. I never told anyone.

Me and Sammy reconciled and moved back in together. We moved to another apartment and were living on third floor. Again, he moved someone in with us and he became even more abusive and disrespectful, bringing women to the house, and doing even more drugs. My daughter got sick and me and my children moved to another apartment. This place was mice and roach infested. It also had mold. I was pregnant with my third daughter and I didn't realize my water broke. I end up delivering her at eight months. She was premature, and I end up moving into a shelter A year later.

I found another place. My third daughter at the time was about a year and a half, I had just found out I was pregnant with my fourth child while I was living on Jersey City.

I moved into this building that was remodeled and just receive my Taxes. I gave Sammy my taxes because he knew the landlord. The landlord had a deal until my TRA started, which is a government assistance program designed to help by paying my rent for the first year, Sammy decided to take my tax money. He met these Jamaicans from down the street, I guess they made a deal and he end up buying a bike and getting a package of drugs for himself.

One evening I came home, I was about six months pregnant. I found Sammy in the closet at the Jamaicans house with red and black candles. I was devastated, and didn't know what was going on but it didn't look right, and I was too tired to even ask questions. I just came from looking for a job, so I could be able to pay all my bills and get furniture. A girlfriend of mine said there's a job opening where I work with children, I said take me there, so I can fill out app and was hired on the spot. I was very excited! I came home and asked Sammy did he pick baby up from daycare center? He told me no, so I left and went to pick up my daughter. The lady at the front desk asked me if it would be okay if I could take pictures of my daughter for a billboard, she was sure my daughter would end up on one of the billboards and buses on an Avenue and my daughter made the billboards. I was so happy.

One evening I came in from work and was very tired and went to visit the lady downstairs. She is a very nice older woman. She had her own issues but said that I was going through a lot. I spent time with her downstairs and she said to me, she asked me "do you know what Sammy does all day while you're not here?" I replied no. He's supposed to be looking for a job. She replied, "oh yes he works but not the type of work you think he's supposed to be doing. I went to my house one day and something didn't seem quite right, the smell hit you right away, I went into my kitchen I seen a whole bunch of N@!#$s in my home again, something just wasn't right. I went in kitchen the asshole was cooking crack! I said where is my baby, did you pick her up from school? He replied yes, she's in the room. The way my house was set up my kitchen and bathroom were connected. I kicked everyone out my house including and went into my bedroom. The baby was feeling very sick and noticed she had drunk her dad's soda. It wasn't soda that nasty mofo pissed in the bottle and my baby drunk it and was throwing up! I had to take her to emergency room and explained what happened to the doctor. Not knowing what's going in my own house as time went on my pregnancy began to increasingly show, the people at my job began asking and if I was pregnant. I couldn't lie. I had to tell her that I was, she said well I must terminate you, I was devastated! I was so tired and so stressed out and I ended up in emergency room.

Sammy came with me. I asked the nurse can you check the baby and the nurse said yes. I can also you tell me the sex of the baby since you're close to your last trimester, he said if it's a girl then that baby is not mine it's your other baby fathers. I know you were cheating on me. I said I never cheated on you

while we were together. He replied your lying. The nurse advised me it was a girl, he just walked out the room. I was crushed. I cried out GOD! I'm tired of going through all this agony. The following day I checked the mailbox and I had a letter from a Housing Authority stating I had two weeks to come and fill out the paperwork to receive Affordable Housing. I was excited. A fresh start is what I needed to get it right. I asked Sammy what is he going to do, is he staying or is he living with me he replied I don't know. I said I'm leaving. He replied I don't care by you ain't taking my kids with you. I called his stepmother and she spoke with him. Whatever she said to him, I guess changed his mind. Now I had to find a way to move to another place. I didn't know the place at it and realize it was six hours away. There's no transportation out there other than a train or plane or greyhound and that took about 18 hours to get there. The older woman from downstairs, huddled me and my children off to

Virginia. She said you could stay with my daughter and catch the greyhound, I replied thank you so much! She replied it's no problem you're like a daughter to me, I was in tears.

Sammy and I reconciled, and we moved and I paid my first deposit for my security deposit. The administrator advised me you must get here to pick up your keys within a week. I'm sitting here trying to find someone who can help me move all the things I just bought for the apartment. I was in and I couldn't find anyone, and time was ticking down. I was so happy my grandfather and great uncle was in town and they were able to take me to the house that we were staying in, just in time for me to get my keys. I was in my new home I was so happy because I had a lot of space and wasn't around a whole bunch of riffraff and I was happy again.

We left behind all that hell and I was moving to our new home and didn't have to worry about people coming to my house, and being in a drug infested area. I don't have to worry anymore. I was living in a new place for just a week when Sammy invited a friend who had nowhere to go to come stay with us.

Here we go yet again! Now I'm about seven months pregnant and he's bringing someone else to live in our house. Our brand-new home. I'm so tired of this and can't even say anything because I never got a chance to. The young man was already on his way. He was a half an hour away.

As time went on Sammy decided to make friends out there, I was in the house with my three children and one on the way. I started getting a lot of pain in my stomach and kept going back-and-forth to the hospital. I thought I was in labor and they said I was just a little stressed. I said ok but for the last couple of weeks, I was in this excruciating pain. Sammy was taking care of me it was around my birthday and one of his friends he met he had him cook for me for my birthday and he brought the food for only one person.

One evening I was in severe pain I couldn't do anything about it and needed to go to the emergency room. I was admitted into the hospital, they admitted me and took a urine test, as well as all the other test that were needed. I was unable to go to the hospital when I lived in New York. The nurse asked me did I do any type of street drugs or anything of the nature, I told her no. I didn't. The nurse came back to me and said that you lied. We found amphetamine in your urine I asked her what is that. She replied street drugs. I said excuse me, you need to check my urine again, I don't take any type of drugs she said well that's not what your test are saying. I hurt once again didn't know how the drugs got into my system. I was so upset. When I got home I waited to the following day and called the hospital and told them to retest me. I couldn't believe it and was so confused I called and told him. When I got home he wasn't there. Finally, he came back to the house his eyes were so glassy and he was acting weird. Throughout my entire relationship with Sammie he constantly verbally. Physically, emotionally, and sexually abusing me. He started biting me and raping me as well because I wouldn't want to have sex with him. It has gotten extremely difficult to live with him. The doctor put me on bed rest, so I had to stay upstairs in my bedroom. My first and second daughter had to help take care of me. Sammy was nowhere to be found. He was running the streets with women and was always over a friend of ours house. I was upstairs and heard Sammy and his friend downstairs. I came downstairs and screamed, what the hell is going on! Sammy and his friend both had women in our home. He tried to get me to believe they were talking. I replied that's not what it looks like. I kicked them all out my house. I don't know where they went and didn't care! I had a doctor's appointment a week later and scheduled a C-section. I couldn't bear the pain any more. I was supposed to have my daughter in February the doctor schedule her appointment for January 27. After I had her he didn't come to the hospital to even check on us. I came home to empty house. My children were over my friend Mary house. I was in my healing process when he came home trying to reconcile. I had my last child, she was in a crib and she's about a week old. We talked and tried to reconcile of course apologized. I will try to work something out. The following day he went to a friend's house and didn't come back home for two days. I told him you I can't worry about this anymore. I had a C-section and I had my tubes tied. I was in a lot of pain, he took all my pain medication and I was left helpless. He came home pissy drunk and tried to lay on top of me. I told him no! He said I don't care I'll just I'll fuck you in the ass and he did! He didn't care that I was in pain. He didn't care about anything. Once again, I was hurt. The baby was crying he was yelling and I was in a lot of pain. I told him he had to leave, and he can't come back so that's what he did. As soon as I start healing, I started school for home health aide to get my life back on track. I started working while I was still in my healing process. I had enough strength to go to school and to work. It just so happened Sammy also was in the same program as I and was attending the same school. He started dating another woman at the school. I was just devastated and intended to totally ignore him. I left school early because I didn't want to deal with the drama with him at school. I started getting phone calls that would just hang up. I knew it was his new girlfriend and I told her I don't know where he is. She just repeatedly calls my number looking for him and asking do I know where he is? I replied you should know where your boyfriend is. I had to get in touch with him because he had my other cell phone and keys to my apartment. I contacted him and said to him that I want my phone and my keys, at this time he was over one of my girlfriend's house hanging out with her with her brother. I went over to my girlfriend's house. She invited me over, so I brought the kids and the baby. When I got there Sammy was there and his new girlfriend. She was talking a whole lot of mess saying I am going to take your man and your baby. I replied really, and things went left quickly. It got heated I ended up fighting in the girl and was beating her so badly, Sammy came outside and jumped on my back and a girl ran. I came in the house and I sat down they handed me the baby, so I had to get up to get comfortable and Sammy came in angry while I was holding the baby he kicked me in my stomach. I wasn't even fully healed and I had the baby in my arms. Talk about excruciating pain and hurt. I've been with this guy for 11 years and this is what he does. They took the baby from out of my arms and I took Sammy into another room. My friend took us to another room and said that we needed to talk. The kids were in the living room people were in the kitchen and some were upstairs. Me and Sammy were sitting across from each other at the dining room table, I said I just want my keys and my phone. He told me, I am not giving you shit at that moment held my left hand and in his right hand he had a blade, and nobody could see what he had in his hand only me. I felt at any moment my life could end. there and I was praying to GOD. I said GOD please get me out the situation. God please come and save me because this man is about to kill me. Fortunately, someone came downstairs and asked are you ok? I replied yeah, I just want to go home.

WHEN I MET KHANN

Finally, I left Sammy and was going through so much. I was very sick. I had my 4 children, no family near me, and no transportation I couldn't even get to the grocery store for necessities.

I was bleeding so bad that I needed a blood transfusion. I had the women down the street watch my children while I was in the hospital she called me a few days later advising me she could no longer watch them. I had to leave and signed myself out the hospital. I was so tired and so stressed.

As soon as my money came in the beginning of the month, I left on the first train smoking out of there and gave all my things away, and came back to our previous apartment. I stayed at my family house. Once I was better I went back to my apartment in Virginia.

I was still living in New York at the time and it was around Labor Day. My family liked this place, Western beef a butcher shop, to get the groceries need to celebrate. That's when I met this guy named KHANN in the store. I looked a hot mess. He was waving me down and I thought he was talking to my friend. He said no, I wanted to talk to you. I asked him why would you want to talk to me, he said I know who I want to talk to, you. I really wasn't looking for anyone at the time, but I didn't mind talking. We went on a few dates and he showed me a good time. he was an older guy at the time I was 27 years old and needed to try something different.

My youngest daughter was about eight months old and I was very depressed sad and not feeling well. I was vulnerable. I just didn't want to stay at my family's home anymore. I didn't have anyone to help me but I still payed my bills. It was nice to be back in my own place with no drama in Pennsylvania. I was feeling a little better about myself.

I thought this man was really the one to help me get through all this pain. I told him I live in Pennsylvania. Will you come and visit me in Pennsylvania? He replied yes, I'll call you every day or come and visit you. I asked really, you would do that? You know how far that is? I live about six hours away.

When I got back home to Virginia I scheduled a doctor's appointment and had to have surgery on the lining of my uterus to stop the bleeding. It was emergency surgery because I was losing so much blood. I had to get blood transfusions back to back and the baby was severely anemic. He came to visit me often and one day unexpectedly after we had been dating for 2 to 3 months he asked to marry me. I was shocked.

We got married and I asked GOD is this true, is this my husband? I did a fast for seven days with just water in hopes that this was really the man for me, and would be good to me for the rest of my life, forever. Though he wasn't my type, beauty is in the eye of the beholder, he was the only person that came out there to visit and check on me so now we're married. He moved in with me in Pennsylvania and helped me a lot. Before we moved back to my Pennsylvania apartment I had to stay with my aunt in the family home in New York to get everything settled in New York. We lived on the third floor and he had been working at his job for about 17 years, we couldn't just get up and go, we had to make proper arrangements before we went back to Virginia.

We all returned to Virginia and everything was going well. I was married, I was in my own place, I had a father figure in the house for my girls and as time went on I was healing and wanted to do something to make me feel appreciated. I decided to go to the gym, my youngest was about 1 and a half at this time and my second child was about six or seven and my oldest wasn't with me. She stayed in New York with my mom.

I was going to the gym and left the two youngest with my husband they were in the living room and my husband was cooking fried chicken before I left. There were times when I came home from the gym, he would give me this strange looking as if he was afraid of me. I said what's wrong, what's going on? He said it's not that bad. I went upstairs to check my babies everything appeared that there's nothing wrong with my third child, but my youngest had a pamper on and from crotch down to the back of her leg in on her stomach was blistered up. I asked him what happened he said the kids were playing in the kitchen and oil fell on her. I took her to the hospital and they said there's no burn unit out in Pennsylvania, so they had to heliport her to Pittsburgh. I had no way of getting there and his truck was not working. I had to ask a friend of mine who lived out there If she would be able to take me to Pittsburgh. I had nowhere to stay in Pittsburgh am my baby was there in agony and pain for almost 3 months. This is how GOD works, they put us in a hotel with the people who were on hospice. Of course, Child Protective Services asked a lot of questions and I gave them the answers. They advised me I couldn't have my husband around my children because he was the person that was there when the accident happened. They ruled the case an accident. I was so hurt and so confused my baby was in the hospital for about 3 months and I didn't tell anyone.

As time went on, I was living in housing and receiving public assistance and it was time for my review. I had to report all income. I did. At least I thought did. I received a letter in the mail advising I had committed fraud. I had to appear in court and lost **all** my benefits. I didn't understand what was going on. then I receive a phone call from my Aunt stating that my husband has mail at the home and it was from child support as well as a check from unemployment. I said What!! He never told me he had children, now my mind is really screwed up. I'm being fined and losing my home and possibly jail time. What more can happen?

They put me on probation and we left Virginia and returned to New York. I had to start all over again. We found place in South Carolina, it was all I could afford at that time. I had all my girls with me. We lived in a two-bedroom apartment, I started going back to work and school. I had two jobs, so we can make ends meet. He was doing transportation at the supermarket. I would leave about 6am and didn't get home until about 7 pm so he was responsible for caring for the girls. Sometimes depending on the schedule my girls came to work with me.

He used to take me to work and pick me up and was usually late hanging out with his identical twin brother but every payday he was always on time. I had to depend on him for everything.

One day I was called to come to school for my second daughter, the guidance counselor asked me has there been any changes at home because my daughter was having a hard time in school. I told her no, we just moved back to New York not too long ago and she also had learning difficulty. The guidance counselor replied ok.

As time went on and he finally introduced me to his daughter who was around the same age as my second daughter. She came by often and it was a pleasure. I was a little embarrassed because my home wasn't up to par and I didn't realize this man was a hoarder. I was raised to be organized and wasn't home enough to teach my children. They had to learn to be independent early and take care of each other.

One day his daughter came and visit, and my second daughter became closer and began confide in her. His daughter's mom advised me to be careful with him around your girls, I said come again? What do you mean by that, she replied just what I said.

About a week later he came to pick me up from work and this time he was super early with my children in the car. He said to me something happened and needed to talk to me because my middle daughter is putting lies about me, saying I touched her. I asked my daughter in front of him did he touch you she said no. I took her word for it and left the situation alone. I started a change in my house hold, I needed a break. One day I said let's go to Jersey City and we went the first time and I won $1,800.00 and was so excited we came come and I paid some bills and got the car fixed and was able to get another car, well at least I thought all the bills were paid. Turns out that we were 3 months behind on rent. Every pay I gave this man my check to pay the bills and never had much for myself. I asked him how'd we get this far in the hole? he replied me he had to get the car fixed. I found out he was gambling with my money, him am his brother ever since I won in Jersey City.

He would force me to go with to the point I was crying and didn't want to go anymore because he was using my money and blowing it. We didn't have food in the house rent wasn't paid cellphone was pass due. He got this crazy idea in his head to start this mailing service and it was a Pyramid fraud. He brought two copy machines and a computer. I said fine if it's going to make money and put food on the table.

I was able to get part time unemployment until I found another job. I end up finding another job about a month later and called to stop the unemployment checks, well at least I thought I stopped them. I didn't see any more checks coming he has been working on this mailing side job and some money came from it so one day he decided to put a $100.00 bill in the copy machine and it duplicated the money so much so that you couldn't tell the difference. He had just got a job at the Prudential Center and came home one day excited he said, remember the hundred dollars I copied, I used it to put gas in the truck. The gas attendant gave me cash back. You can probably guess what happened next. I failed to tell this man you are supposed to be GOD fearing man but the only time he went to church was when he needed something or help. I'm so confused right now! He is doing the nothing Godly men are supposed to do.

I was at work on day and my cellphone was off, he picked me up on time and was very excited. He told me a check came for me in the mail, it was my last unemployment check. We went to Bank of America and cashed the check. It wasn't a lot it was just enough to get use through the week. I thought it was my last check to find out they were coming the whole and he was signing them and deposited the in our joint account. I found out about the unemployment checks when I received a letter stating I owe the government back pay. I did my taxes and didn't get my refund check because I owed them.

I was so angry, the following week he picked me up from work and said to me GOD is good, he blessed us. I asked what you mean by that, he didn't tell me my phone was off again and he dropped me off home and told me he will be right back. An hour passed and heard banging on my door. It was the police yelling open up, of course I did. The police to me to put your hands up and drew guns on me and my children. They showed me a picture and asked me if I knew this man? I said yes, that's is my husband. They asked me do I know his where about? I replied no, I just got off work. The police asked me when was the last time you seen him. I replied about an hour ago. The officer said I need to check the house because my husband stole $10,000 from the bank, I was floored. I let them check the house they finally withdrew their guns. They didn't find anything. The officer said they will be looking for him. I said to him fine. About a few hours later he showed up and I nearly flipped my wig. I asked him where were you, I was trying to reach you? He didn't reply. The police came drew gun on me and the kids. In my head I was done so he told me what happened and turned himself in to the police department.

The irony, the money he took from the bank was from a pastor, it was tithing money. The pastor didn't press charges his only requirement was for him to bring us to his place of worship. and we went we got to the church and the pastor greeted me and my family and gave him $50.00 to take me and the kids to dinner. We never made it to dinner, but he made sure he made in to Jersey City. Now I am just so lost for words.

I was going through changes at my job and I was just tired of looking for a way out, one day I was at a different site that turned out to become the permanent place for me. My supervisor was a very nice. She was an ex drug addicted who hired the strangest people. To get the message to me she said I don't know why I am telling you this but start catching the bus don't rely on your husband. She started to give me more hours, so I can make more money, she even helped me get a bus card. She said to me be careful with your daughters around him. I said what, why did you say that? She told me something isn't right with him. All I could do was listen. I started catching the bus to work and was working at two sites.

Things where flowing very well, it was tax season again and we needed to move. My mom was living in New York. I put in applications for her complex and my credit was in good condition so as soon as I received my taxes I signed the lease and did not include him and didn't even tell him I had the place I did everything with my mom's help. I went back to the old place and said to him I am taking the kid, I need some time to myself. We are not in a good place right now, when I'm ready I will call you, by that time I was already in my new place. I never gave him a key and he didn't even know where I lived, until his cousin seen me and told him where I stayed.

I had already filed for divorce and it took about 2 years. I was waiting on that. I went back to school and got a second job, so I can make sure all my bills will be paid. I was by myself for a while and needed a break. Six months passed, and I was working on myself and trying to find some type of normalcy. It was tax season again, I took some of my money and put it toward bills and a vacation to Jamaica for the summer.

WHEN I MET EDWIN

I was heading to work waiting at the bus stop running late, when this older gentleman stopped me his name was Edwin. He offered me a ride to work.

I waiting for the 99 bus I was running super late God had put me in a position at my second job my cousin wife was my supervisor and she treated me fair when she was in a good mood so I called her when I was late and she told me I can make the time up later on in the week. As I was waiting for the bus, I wasn't paying attention to the cars around me my focus was the bus, I saw the bus it was a way down the street. I was preparing to get ready when Ed was in the parking lot and yelled to me to get my attention. He called me beautiful and then asked me for my number. I told him my bus is coming so I hurried up and gave him my number, jumped on the bus. Before I turned the corner, the guy said I would take you to work get off at the next stop, so I did. I got in the car and got to work about ten minutes late instead of a half hour late. I thanked him he asked if he could call me later and I told him of course. He asked me can he pick me up from work, I told him I have a few things to do. He said I will take you where you need to go, I would like to get to know. He took me where I needed and was very kind, mature, very patient and catered all my needs. He was there for me i.e. picking me up from work, helping me with some miscellaneous items, taking me grocery shopping, and to the laundromat. He never came on to me in a sexual way. I was relieved about it. I was very comfortable because I was still going through my divorce and I had legal trouble because of my husband and at that time I wasn't ready to get into a relationship. I was looking for a friend at the time and that is what Edwin was. I was going through a lot. I often had panic attacks and anxiety attacks. One day I received a letter that there was a warrant for my arrest in Pennsylvania for nonpayment of a fine, and I burst out in tears. He asked me what was wrong, and I didn't say anything, so he held me, and he was comforting me once again. I never had someone treat me so nice and understanding. I didn't bring him around my children. We were talking about 6 months and within that time I was about to lose my place because I wasn't making enough money. My electricity bill was very expensive, and I had no food in the house. I couldn't even do my laundry and my children were out of order. I was losing faith in GOD and just kept feeling like I was being punished. I was in this weird space in my life. I was venting and had a panic attack and Edwin was by my side, so he prayed for me. I was shocked he was a GOD-fearing man. Wow, that made me feel a whole lot better. He had his on situation going on and I was there for him like he was there for me. It came to the point where I introduced him to my children and he came in my home and stayed a few nights, he brought groceries and he helped me cleanup. He washed my walls down, he helped me get my children in line and I never even had sex with this man. He even helped put some light in my house, so I felt ok to open up to him and I did let him know I am waiting for my divorce. He helped me with that he said he didn't want to commit adultery. I was fine with that. We got to a point in the relationship that we were reading the Bible together and I am thinking everything is going well. My children seemed to be ok with him and I felt safe. a year had passed and finally, my divorce was final 3 days after my birthday I was very happy as a few months went by I was really struggling where I was staying and ended up getting evicted. I tried everything to keep my place going to all the resources that were available to me through the government. I ended up having a nervous breakdown. I and my children ended up living with my mom and my stepfather who lived across the court from me in a two-bedroom apartment. It wasn't the easiest thing to do. I felt worthless and it didn't get better. Edwin came to see me as often as he could. He had his on situation going on I never really asked because he was my concern. My children, my babies were struggling in school and I had to get them evaluated. I didn't realize they were having a hard time until the school social worker called me in for a meeting. Now I am even more overwhelmed. My children are struggling in school, they need clothes. I had no money, I had to leave work so now I was receiving welfare because I couldn't work in my condition and I was living with my parents. One day Edwin came to see me, and he took me to a place to get me and my babes some clothes, he took us to the Salvation Army family store. I was relieved. I am asking myself why this man is being so nice. One day he came to visit me at my mom's house and I had these pants on, I guess it showed too much of my figure and he didn't approve. He had an attitude and ripped my pants to where I was unable to where them. I was really confused. He said no woman of mine will dress like that. I was covered and didn't get it. Then he said why are the kids sleeping on the floor? He said I need to get you out of here and told and he told me he was working on something. I was at my wits end. I decided to go to welfare and get into a shelter. I left my mom's house and ended up in a shelter, and my children were in their own beds and I had my on space. We attended church and the kids were in the afternoon school program and they were happy, but I know it was temporary, so I started to seek counseling for me and my babies and Edwin came to visit us often, but he was not allowed to come in the shelter because of the safety of the other women and children. The only way is through court order stating that he is me and my children's caregiver, so that's what we did at least that is what I thought anyway. As time went on he was able to come in the shelter and he spent a lot of time with us. we were in the shelter for about 6 months and it started to feel like jail even though we had a place it wasn't my own. I started to go to a program for myself to get help. I ended up seeing a psychiatrist and they put me in a day program where I was diagnosed with PTSD severe depression anxiety and panic attacks. I took a lot of medicine. Now I am approaching the 7 months in the shelter and I was able to file my last taxes, so I did, and Edwin said we can buy a bigger car and we can start doing transportation. Of course, I was like why not. I took my taxes and bought the 2007 suburban and l bought him a Rolex watch because he said it will help him get high end clients because of the type of transportation he was doing. Now we were approaching 8 months and I received a letter stating I will be getting a check and my third child she will be getting SSI because she has a disability. They sent me a check as well because they said I also was disabled. I was approaching 9 months and my time was up in the shelter, so I had to find another place to stay. I went back to the complex I used to live in and ended up living next door to my mother. Edwin and I were officially together, and the children were in a one-bedroom apartment and I felt like I can breathe again. I had a monthly income coming in and someone to help me with my children, so now me and Edwin are together, and he was coming in the house every day around 2am in the morning like clockwork. He didn't have consistent clients, and he wasn't working. I paid all the bills. He didn't have much money so I asked him where do you go early in the morning and what kind of work that keep you late at night or at least until 2 am very night. He told me that was none of my business, I need to stay in my place. and do my motherly duties. He also told me don't worry about what he is doing, just know I am bringing money in the house. One evening he left his iPad home and what I saw was quite disturbing. My heart was broken, and I was crying all night. I asked him about it and he yelled and screamed at me it was very uncomfortable to be in the same room with him. Now I am trying to stay calm. Months went by and I received a letter from NEWARK HOUSING AUTHORITY stating my number was up for a 3-bedroom apartment. I was so happy. We ended up moving before the year was out. Now we are in our new place and the kids had their own room and we are doing very well. I thought we were in a good place in our relationship. I was very confused because he has become very mean and very controlling to the point I was crying every day. I was receiving a lot he paid all the bills with my card and I bought him another car because we were starting our own luxury car company service. I was on board with that. As time went on he came to me and asked me was it ok if his sister stayed with us. I said off course, I don't mind he said she can help us out and food and bills. I was on board with his sister staying with us only find out, that was not his sister but his ex-girlfriend I was speechless. I found out her who she was I was when I was talking to her. I was hurt to say the least. I'm really looking at him sideways now. Time went on and his sister/ ex-girlfriend found her own place and my house was somewhat back to normal. One day my second oldest daughter came home from school and she didn't seem herself, I asked her was she ok she told me yes then An hour later I get a knock on the door and it was social service saying that we are under investigation because my daughter's claims that her stepfather (my ex-husband) had sexually molested her and I just hit the floor. I was so hurt confused and asked her who and she said KHANN. I was hurt because I couldn't protect her, she said that the only man at the time who was a father figure was Edwin. I asked her is it him, but she said it was my ex-husband and I was simply lost for words. As time went by we were cleared from the investigation and the case was closed. I decided all my children including myself would need to seek help. Edwin saw to it that we made it to each appointment and he made a few friends on the way. He was able to keep an eye on us. They would report back to him with our progress we made. He made sure he was watching my every move. I didn't understand why he was that way, one day I was sick, and I ended up in the hospital for a week. I told him to take my girls to my mom's house, he did except one and that was my second oldest. I didn't know it at the time. I was wondering why later when I found out. I didn't think too much about it. While healing from the Surgery I had, I was very weak and vulnerable. He took care of me and I noticed that him and my second eldest was becoming very close. I asked him about that he said because she has been talking to him and trusting him. I told him I don't play favorites in my home, he said I love all your children but he started treating my children differently it seems like he didn't like my youngest and my third child he treated her different to and he was doing this for a while and he started to treat my second eldest as his woman and me like one of the children. I was confused about what was happening. He started threatening me, he kept fire arms under his pillow and became more abusive. I wanted to kill myself on so many occasions. We've been in a relationship for about 5 to 6 years, and I was ready to get out. I just didn't know how. We were struggling once again and lost the business. His ex-girlfriend moved back in because she was having a hard time as well and everything was just out of control. This is how I know GOD was in the mist. When his ex-girlfriend came back to live with us, she helped me with a lot of things and whatever he said to her about me, she told me that he was nothing like what he said he was. She became of great value in my life. One of my favorite Aunt's was talking to me and we were getting on the prayer line three days out of the week, I needed an outlet a lot of things was coming to head my Aunt was leaving to move to New Jersey. She was telling me about it for a while and there was still a lot going on. I was saying to myself, I always wanted to live in New Jersey. As time went by my second eldest was getting sick and was not her normal self. One day she told me she was pregnant, and I said what? By whom? She said by some boy she knew in school, whom didn't have a phone and moved to West Virginia. I was lost! I asked her what do you want to do, and she said to get rid of it. I have my whole life ahead of me. we took her to get an abortion. I was just baffled about the whole thing then she started having complications after that. I was back in forth in the emergency room and I asked because something didn't make since. I ask her has Edwin touched you in any way? She told me no, she said he is not that kind of guy. As time went on he became more aggressive and we had a big fallout my eldest daughter came by to see me and introduce me to her new boyfriend. Edwin was not too fond of her. He wouldn't let me open my front door for her, I had to go to the back door. I felt horrible and just wanted to escape. I started saving up money he used to give me from my check, and I started to prepare to move. I opened another bank account and I stopped telling him everything. Things started getting really crazy in my home. I asked one of my other Aunts for some Anointing oil, so I can bless my home. I told him about the oil and he took that oil and rubbed it on my feet trying to be funny. What he didn't know he just bought me a new pair of shoes. He took the oil and poured it out directly in front of the front door. I said thank you. What he didn't know he gave me a way out. Time went on and we had gotten into a really bad fight. He threatened me with the guns. Hit me with a piece of wood broken off my second eldest daughter door, all because I wasn't letting him separate me and my children. I wanted to go to my mom's house for Mother's Day, he said I can go bot only with my two youngest daughters. My second eldest was staying with him. I told him no she isn't, and we had a big fight about that too. I was just so tired and done! I couldn't take it anymore! I tried to kill myself. As I was doing this GOD said to me if you kill yourself how can I help you. I thought I was going crazy. I took the belt from around my neck and took a nap. I woke up and had a new mind set. I figured out how to escape and GOD made it to where everything was in line. I was covered with his precious blood. As punishment he used to take my cell phone away and cut the service off. My Aunt suggested I get another cell phone he doesn't know about and tell no one. I did. One day I took my cell phone and my second daughter's cell phone and got rid of them. My eldest daughter took the cell phone and tried to sell them, but she couldn't since she needed the password. It had to be cleaned out. When my eldest daughter got the phone opened she was shocked! She couldn't believe what she was seeing and hearing. She called me immediately, she was very angry and disgusted.

WHEN WE RAN FROM EDWIN

We had to run away from Edwin to August GA, when we were finally settled and found out the information regarding my daughter and Edwin, I immediately went to social service and advised the authorities what was going on to get justice my daughter. Now my daughter was acting out and very angry with me, she didn't understand what was taking place. It was time for me to have a heart to heart with her. I let her know that I went through her phone and I saw a lot of messages and videos of inappropriate and Disgusting vile things that hurt me to my core. I asked her some questions because something didn't feel right in my spirit and we talked for a while and she answered all the questions. The last question took everything out of me, I asked her who was the person that got you pregnant? She told me, Edwin. My heart dropped, angry was an understatement! I was broken tremendously, I didn't protect my babies. I felt worthless. I did everything possible to make things right and went through the proper channels to get my family help and he still found out where we ended up and was able to brain wash her even more to the point that my baby was plotting against me to get me locked up. I can't blame her because I didn't protect her, and he had a stronghold only GOD could break. My baby ran a way and my family was working around the clock to get her back. She was gone for weeks, it felt like death every second out of the day. My baby was home with me my family gotten the SVU FBI went on Facebook gotten the news reporter involved special OPS they went above and beyond to find her. When I finally got my baby back, she was home for a few days and I had to get her committed because she hated me so much and had every right to be because of all that she went through was enough to feel insecure and untrusting towards me. The police said that they found her. I was in New York getting a restraining order towards Edwin because he was the cause of her disappearance. We found her Alabama. Let me tell you how GOD works. I was in our previous apartment pressing charges against everything he had done to me and my family as well waiting to see the judge in court for the finalization of the restraining order. I was in court and had to appear in court and to make matter worse, I'm here without a restraining order and he requested a restraining order against me, at the time they were still searching for my daughter. I did not know that he was talking to the people in Augusta New Jersey, the police, sheriff's office in New Jersey to make it look like he's not the person who manipulated her to Alabama, all this was happening while we were in court and mind you I have not seen this man's since I left he made sure that he was in the clear. While I was doing the finalization in the court they reported to me that my daughter was found. I went back to New Jersey and had to find a way to get my daughter from Alabama since the authorities gave me a 24-hour period and no financial assistance to help bring her home. I called friends and family and did not know what to do. My mother, aunt, daughter, and my son-in-law drove 12 hours to get here and pick my daughter from Alabama. She was finally home in my arms. I was so happy and at the same time, I was so sad. We just moved into a new place I just found out my eldest daughter was pregnant, and it was a hard process. Everything that was going on GOD provided a new home for me and my children. We were settling in about a week later my daughter started acting out and threaten to hurt her sisters and it was chaos in my home. I couldn't rest because I didn't know what to do. Thank GOD! I had a psyche appointment and I explained to the Doctor what had happened. They asked me do we need to call a 1013 on her. I didn't know at the time what that meant. The doctor explained to me what it was. I was undecided. The doctor start talking to my daughter to see was it safe for her to come home. The doctor advised me to take her the hospital and the will stay on the phone until we arrive there. They admitted her, and she had to stay there for 5 days. When she came home it was hard for her to adjust. It was recommended for her to go to outside facilities. We were following the doctor's orders when one day I received a phone call advising me she can no longer attend this facility. It was due to a conflict of interest. The counselor on staff was a related to me. I did not know he had also relocated to Augusta GA as well, and his wife could not treat her and unfortunately, she was the only counselor there. I was shocked, to say the least, and I hadn't seen my cousin since we were children, and to find out he was also a minister. I asked him can he pray over me and my family and bless my home,

he was blessing my home when a neighbor across the court from me came out of know where knocking on my door and gave my cousin a message. It was powerful and wonderful at the same time. Time went on and my cousin visited me every chance he got. One day he asked me is there a place that I know where we can have bible study. I said no, but I will help you find a place. I offered my home and the ministry has been flowing with great expectation. The devil was mad, and things started happening and one day I had no food, no money, and no one could help me. I called everyone I knew. I had no one to help get one of my younger children to the doctor. I needed a ride. I heard a big BOOM! I was about to give up when I found out the boom was an earth quack. I was shocked! I headed in the house I felt hurt and defeated and as I was going upstairs GOD said for me to turn around and ask the lady downstairs for help. This young lady use to come upstairs to bible study in my home and I don't know her from a can of paint, but she opened her door and her home to me and my children and took me to the doctor and to a food pantry. Can you say amen!! As we were at the food pantry she asked me would I like to go to an event at her church, so we did. It was awesome! I was able to give a little of my testimony. They asked my family to come back and we did. It became a little uncomfortable. I didn't know why we went a few times, but it wasn't for me and my family. We started back where my family is supposed to be and that is where we will remain. Time went on and my children started seeking counsel elsewhere and GOD told me to start my own family therapy in my home and create a war room. I was obedient, and my children were better for it. and they even invited their friends to come and sit in. Things were going great until it was becoming a problem with the management in the complex. I found a new place and it is much better and more spacious. I thank GOD every day for it. Now we are in our new home and we have been here for months and one evening I was asleep and GOD came and to visit me in my sleep. I didn't even know it was GOD. I was rebuking him and everything. I was scared out of my mind, until HE said I am the ALPHA and OMEGA. The beginning and The end. The horned of the heavens where playing and the light was bright, then I woke up I couldn't believe GOD came to visit me. I tried to rebuke him and opened my eyes and turned over looked at the time and went back to sleep and my life as of right now has never been the same.

WHAT MAKES YOU HAPPY

Are you happy
Can you be happy with yourself
Are you capable of making someone else happy
Do you know who holds the key to happiness
How does happiness keep you youthful
How can you spread happiness
How can you recognize happiness
Do you know when you are truly happy
What is the key to your happiness? Do you understand what is happiness is
Are you able to make yourself happy
Do you know how to self-motivate
Do you take responsibility of your own actions
Can you accept your faults Yesterday's past can keep you moving forward? Happiness doesn't make
you happy. It's the journey along the way and the memories that brought you to that decision you
made that brought joy in your life. Joyful noise, a fragrance, home cooking, a special event or just
something as simple as a phrase that someone dear to your heart said to you. A hug or a kiss, there's
nothing like an unconditional love. The feelings you get when you feel that warm Spiritual feeling
in your heart and you don't even know what triggered it. just look up and say thank you LORD
because HE whom is the ALPHA and the OMEGA, HE is the beginning and the end,
HE is love because HE gave his only begotten son to save us all. We need faith the size of
a mustard seed. Can you look in the Mirror and feel confident within yourself
Can you see yourself cry in the mirror
Do you feel you have to cover yourself up because you don't feel pretty or handsome enough.
Do you love yourself?
How do you know?

DO YOU KNOW YOURSELF

What do you know about yourself
What makes you happy
What can you bring to the table for yourself
Are you ambitious
Can you motivate yourself when you are down
Do you have will-power to not subject yourself that can get you to become an addiction
Do you have a low self-esteem
Do you have high self-esteem
Are you Confident
Do you have self-control
Are you happy with yourself

DECODING YOUR INNER HURT

Finding the seed that has nurtured the pain that caused the hurt
And what fed the root that became so prideful that you refused to let go of the one thing that makes
you feel that you can't forgive or has such a strong hold on you that it became part of you.
Are you willing to do Spiritual open heart surgery to get rid of that cancerous disease
of a seed that is holding you back from love, forgiveness and blessings.
Are you too prideful too seek help for healing your heart and breaking the chains of all strongholds on
your life and every empty space within you, that you haven't even realize the hold it has on you.
Are you ready to decode your hurt and reconstruct your life for the better, think differently, talk
differently, walk differently do the things that will better benefit you without changing your
true self but better yourself in ways people will look at you differently and respectfully in a ways
that you never thought you could be respected people will see you in a different light.
Decoding your inner hurt is a journey because you will have to face the skeleton(s) in your
closet and come to terms that you cannot change your past but you can learn from it take
your past as a lesson and an experience in your life and stand strong in your present and
steadfast for your future it not easy for anyone, you are not alone, you are no longer a victim
and we all need a support system rather it's a person music or spiritual guidance.

WHAT IS YOUR ROCK BOTTOM

Who are you using as your crutch
What are you afraid of.
Why are you afraid?
What is success to you?
What makes you successful?
How can you get to your success?
Are you ready to let go of that crutch and be confident within yourself ?
Can you walk in your truth and be self-assured that you can make
it no matter what your situation appears to be?
Are you able to walk by faith and not by sight ?
Can you trust GOD and believe he can do all things if you give your trust and faith in him?
Remember GOD is universal and he whom trust HIM can bank on a feed-back rather it be good bad or
indifferent can you use GOD as your crutch or are you so afraid of your own success with a helping hand
from the spirit of the LORD that gives unconditional love and you are to blinded by what you see and
what you hear and what you can taste and touch and then you wonder why are you still at rock bottom
and it seems endless because of your own self-righteousness and pride but you're still in that same circle and
wondering why am I still here in the same circumstances that looks like a maze but it's an illusion because
you only see your 5 senses where does your rock bottom lye you can make a decision you have a choice you
know right from wrong knowing is forgiving knowing is a choice to make a decision you your future.

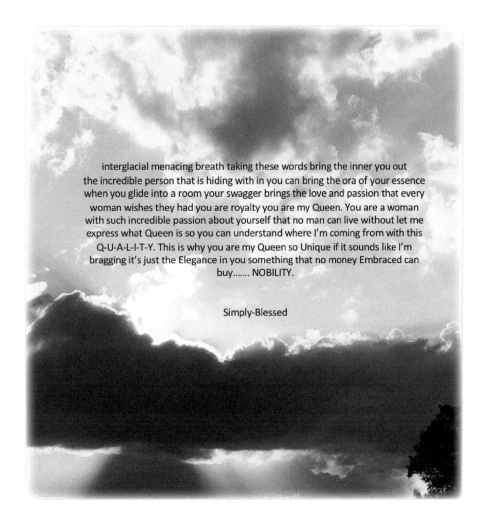

interglacial menacing breath taking these words bring the inner you out
the incredible person that is hiding with in you can bring the ora of your essence
when you glide into a room your swagger brings the love and passion that every
woman wishes they had you are royalty you are my Queen. You are a woman
with such incredible passion about yourself that no man can live without let me
express what Queen is so you can understand where I'm coming from with this
Q-U-A-L-I-T-Y. This is why you are my Queen so Unique if it sounds like I'm
bragging it's just the Elegance in you something that no money Embraced can
buy....... NOBILITY.

Simply-Blessed

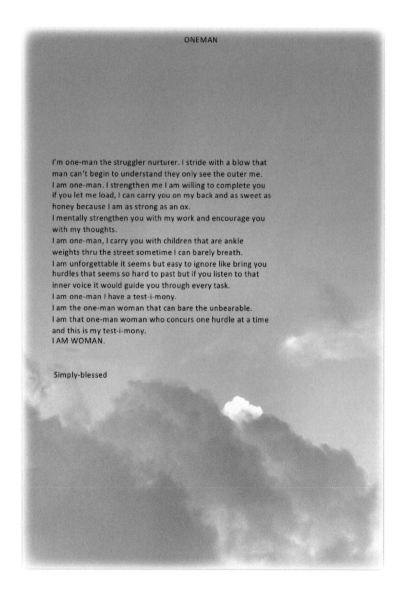

ONEMAN

I'm one-man the struggler nurturer. I stride with a blow that
man can't begin to understand they only see the outer me.
I am one-man. I strengthen me I am willing to complete you
if you let me load, I can carry you on my back and as sweet as
honey because I am as strong as an ox.
I mentally strengthen you with my work and encourage you
with my thoughts.
I am one-man, I carry you with children that are ankle
weights thru the street sometime I can barely breath.
I am unforgettable it seems but easy to ignore like bring you
hurdles that seems so hard to past but if you listen to that
inner voice it would guide you through every task.
I am one-man I have a test-i-mony.
I am the one-man woman that can bare the unbearable.
I am that one-man woman who concurs one hurdle at a time
and this is my test-i-mony.
I AM WOMAN.

Simply-blessed

IS IT TRUE

Is it true the only way a guy can love me is by seeing the anatomy of my body, the vernacular of my tongue and the curves of my Gluteus Maximus? Just to hold a conversation? Is it true? Is the less cloths I wear when a man can see me best? Is it true? GOD is it true the only males that are left in this Millennial Generation would rather have a woman that can care for them while they crave to be bottled fed by their mother's breast? Is it true? GOD is it true that they no longer fear you because the corruption of messages spoken by those you have given charge as men of GOD, who took advantage of your message and turned it into their own? Is it true? GOD is it true that these mothers coddle them because there are no fathers in the homes? GOD is it true they are taking you out the picture because they no longer want your presence and teachings in the Schools? Is it true? LORD why don't they see that you are the only father they need in their lives GOD it True?

SELFISHNESS AND SELFLESSNESS

I was selfish about love.
I was selfish with my heart.
I was selfish with myself.
I was selfish by not caring enough for someone else feeling and emotions.
I was selfish for not taking time seriously.
I was selfish for not trusting god with my fear.
I was selfish for not spreading the word of God when it was needed.
I selflessly given up my wants.
I selflessly given up my likes.
I selflessly give my unconditional love for GOD to many people.
I selflessly given up my love for worldly things to serve GOD.
I selflessly give up my temple just to the person GOD has ordained just for me.
I selflessly give up my time.
I selflessly given up my pride.
I selflessly give up my home to whom need to lay there head for rest.
I selflessly will give my plate to feed a child or a person whom hasn't eaten and is in need of food.
I selflessly give up my needs and sacrifice to protect my love ones.
I selflessly have given up my worldly spirit to become one with GOD.

BREAKING THE CHAIN OF FEAR

Fear you can't have me I am asking GOD to break the yoke.
Fear you can't have my heart I am asking GOD to Break the chain.
Fear you can't have my love I am asking God to break the stronghold. Fear
you can't have my children I given my children to GOD.
Fear you can't have my success I put that in JESUS hands.
Fear you can't have my career because it is protected by GOD.
Fear you are no longer a factor in my life.
The only spirit I Fear is GOD.

WHEN A MAN CRIES

It takes great man to get on his knees and pray to GOD and be God fearing.
It takes a great man to be obedient and disciplined in the word.
It take a great man to show his feelings.
It takes a great man to uplift his family.
It take great man to love unconditionally.
It takes a great man to do whatever it takes to provide for his family no matter what his
situation or circumstance you are more than a great man you are a blessing.

LOVE LANGUAGE

With the dialect of my love language and the spirit in my belly and the passion in my heart one can misunderstand the love that comes through me that is so strong that it can become utterly the most desirable to the person that is lacking that nutrients that is pure-love the spiritual being that is in your circumference this how much I love for GOD and with his DNA running through my veins I pour that out genuinely to whomever is seeking unconditional love peace and serenity that we all desire the compassion and mercy of GOD's grace the favor that was put upon my life this is a great blessing to give once or many times in our journey.

DAILY AFFIRMATION

You are strong.
You are kind.
You are sweet.
You have grace.
You have mercy.
You have favor.
You are loved.
And it is an honor to know YOU and your glory circle people that is near and dear to you.
let your spirit be at peace and your smile brighten the room let your presence be made known and your faith be your strength let GOD fulfill your harvest as it becomes fruitful with great blessing and endless fruit your trial may not be over but your deliverance will come sooner than you expected your heart is pure your love is breath taking and your graduation is near and you will have your heart's desires.

CAN I LEARN TO TRUST AGAIN

Hummm see it's hard because if you have not matured and still have envy for the person or people that have hurt you manipulated you and betrayed you in any away they cut you so deep that you can't sew it stitch it nor staple it and time is taking for ever to heal and you can't seem to forgive the person or people whom as damaged you then guess what they have already won they took your freedom and carrying it like you are a slave and every chance they get they're whooping you with belt of pride that hurt you don't want to let go so you can learn to love and trust again well to let the past be the past and that burden give it to GOD because that hurt no longer belongs to you give up that lease to my new landlord and decide to let the courts of CHRIST handle that sentence yes I am willing to and able to trust again and to love again because I put all my trust in GOD and he is loves and I knows HE has unconditionally love for me. So yes I can love and try again I cast all my fears to love and trust again to my HOLY FATHER he won't leave me of forsake me and I can bank on HIS forgiveness so yes I can love and trust again.

What about you?

Can you love again?

Can you trust again?

Are you willing to let your past be your past?

Are you willing to let your guard down and let someone love you back?

Are you ready to release your burden and care upon GOD?

Are you willing to let go of that pride?

Are you willing to release the same love that is given to you?

Are you willing to trust yourself to be a better you?

Are you ready trust yourself to make better decisions?

Are you ready to graduate from what is holding you back?

THE CHILD WHO WAS LOST

There was this child who couldn't understand why things kept going wrong. This child kept getting in trouble always being blamed for things whether if they were responsible or not, the child kept hanging with the wrong crowd. Then he/she started doing drugs, drinking, had a bad attitude didn't care about their appearance, always lying about the smallest things, had a negative attitude about everything and everyone. The child was hurt, confused and had been thrown out on the streets after the mother had given birth. He/she had been thrown in the system, raped, abused, and sold as a sex slave. He/she dropped out of school. The child was lost, uneducated and lacked structure. No guidance, no one to tell them I love you. The child was lost and cried every day and asked why is this happening to me, why no one can love me, why was I born just to be thrown away? Then as the child was crying on their knees, the child couldn't take it anymore. Sometimes it's the journey and all its tragedies, the child heard the name JESUS CHRIST and GOD but did not know how or what it was since he/she had never been taught only in passing. Through this child's journey, he/she has seen people praying. The child decided to try it because he/she was tired. The child was on his/her knees crying and repeated what was heard by other people, so the child didn't know that they were praying, the child didn't know it was in front of GOD's temple and as the child was crying and praying the child passed out. It hasn't eaten in a long time. The angels of GOD heard the child's cry's and brought the child to the temple. The child had woken up and didn't know how where they were, and it ended up at this place of worship. There was a man that was ordained by GOD himself who was an ancestor of Abraham and said to this child I have been waiting for you. The child was confused, the man of GOD started to minister. This child was so pleased just to be in a safe haven that this child ended up being baptized. The child found what true was love through the word of GOD and the child was no longer lost. This child is now loved and found and spreading the word through the testimony of the journey that GOD has provided for his child. He realized and recognized that true happiness and unconditional love exists in the love of GOD.

WHAT SCARES YOU

What scares you from growing?
What scares you from earning?
What scares you from seeking guidance?
What scares you from your own success?
What scares you from Spiritual guidance?
What scares you to love yourself?
What scares you to love someone else?
What scares you from healing?
Why are you scared?
Do you want to be scared?
Can you heal from what you are scared of?
Do you know why you are scared?
Are you too scared to love and trust?
My love for you is unconditional.

GO ON A DATE WITH YOUR FIRST LOVE

This instruction is very important.
1.) Put your best dressed outfit on.
2.) Find the most private place where you and your first love can be one.
3.) pour your best Glass of Water or Wine.
4.) Set the mood with your best spiritual music.
5.) Snuggle up with the living Word and explore some truth love and prosperity.
6.) Then get one your knees and have a conversation with your first love.
7.) You thank your first Love for the Best Date ever and make sure you
often Date your first love Jesus Christ he is our everything.

P.S. Your First Love should Jesus Christ don't just call on him when you need him rely on him for
everything Date him often show him how much he is worth in your life don't use him as a tool
If you can love a your children a spouse a family member and go above and beyond
then you should be able to love God 1000 time more then you love people and
things of the world because without God these things has no value.

Hebrews 7:25 KJV; Wherefore he is able also to save them to the uttermost that come unto God by him, seeing he ever liveth to make intercession for them.

Romans 8:28 KJV; And we know that all things work together for good to them that love God, to them who are the called according to his purpose.

NEVER

Never feel guilty because of the hand that was dealt to you
forgiveness is the key.
Decisions you make becomes an experience.
And the best lessons that is taught.
Don't let your pride Intervene
and your guilt because you can easily lose your blessings that is waiting for you in the present future
become humble understand what is what and what his wants and what is need in life it can make your
decision is much easier for you. I am a keyholder. I am much more valuable more than my flesh. I
am a child of God. I try to keep my spirit clean, stay true to myself, trust God, my body is a valuable
and not to be disrespected. I love unconditionally forgive myself and the ones that hurt me.
I declare I decree that GOD has all power there is no one before HIM or after HIM no idle should be
praised no man should be praised always shop put God first in your life and no he shall supply all your
needs to his riches in glory through Christ Jesus you are a virtuous woman and you must be humble
within yourself never be vain never be too proud do not let your pride get your way. We are heirs of the
king, the blood, the love is the LORDS. We are the products of our ancestors, we have a chance in life
to do better than our ancestors and take the good values installed within us and put them to work.
My help meet is going to find me I don't have to go looking for him. Nor Chase after
him, I put my trust in GOD HE will bring me and help me become a virtuous woman
and bring me a Spiritual soulmate that GOD specifically pick just for me.
And when that man finds his virtuous wife, he will be blessed beyond his imagination.
A man whom seek his wife finds a great being because that women will help
strengthen him when he falls weak and help rebuild his Vertebrae.
Bone by bone and encourage him, not disable him. she will comfort him and nurture his spirit and
the Man will treat her as his queen and they will become one. Be patient and don't rush for nothing,
be kind and love unconditionally, forgive and be humble and don't let pride take your blessings,

Romans 8:28 KJV; And we know that all things work together for good to them that love God, to them who are the called according to his purpose.

1 Corinthians 13:13 KJV; And now abideth faith, hope, charity, these three; but the greatest of these is charity.

TRAUMA

Trauma it holds you back it has you devastated
It can make you believe a lie and have you thinking you high and make you
self-medicated on just on the unknown Pharmaceuticals that
keep you blind, Lethargic, Hallucinating, and looking like anthrax sent an attack every part
of your mind body and Spirit. Life is at a standstill. Lost in time, whining about the questions
that never can be answered (WHY?), then you start unfolding, composing and still wondering
(WHY?) because the traumatic concerns of other people thoughts of you, their unknown pain
for you and hurt want you to have no brain of your own and then imply things to make it look
like it's all your thoughts. Can you ask yourself the Vulnerable Question (WHY) me?
Why is this happening once again with the meth running through your head and veins like a maze making
sound decision on other people's opinions for your life and decisions they want you to have using their
brain and not your own as if you were their puppet and you don't know right from wrong. They are too
scared to stand up for themselves, so they use you as a tool in their inbox that they built because they have
the Christopher Columbus effect that would have you steal kill and destroy to claim it as their own.
Pain doesn't last. Time heals all wounds. Time is more precious and more valuable then you know. Time
teaches patience. Time is something you should not waste. Once it's gone it's gone and you can't get it back.
The best thing about time is it doesn't stop, and you have many chances to make corrections for yourself,
it gives you plenty of opportunities. The only thing that can stop time is when you stand still and GOD is
talking to you and brings you home to be loved by many and hated by most, but that doesn't bother you
because they're still trying find what you have just learned. Time and love works hand and hand learn from
the past and bring positive things energy to your new fruitful harvest looking forward to new beginning.

2 Corinthians 5:17 KJV; Therefore if any man be in Christ, he is a new creature:
old things are passed away; behold, all things are become new.

FOOD FOR THOUGHT

Yesterday is a lesson.
Today is a great blessing.
Tomorrow's is a new beginning into your journey.
Life is too short-lived not to enjoy every minute second of it once you put God first your journey will always have a great story along the way and within your path, you will find your self-ministering to some whom needs unconditional love along the way keep your eye on the prize and know God speaks life in us we don't speak life in God but we can spread his word and show his love that he in steeled within us.

Holy Bible

H*He
O*Only
L*Left
Y*You

B*Basic
I*Instruction
B*Before
L*Leaving
E*Earth

THE MOMMY GUILT

When you want your children to do better than you and as they are growing up you try to correct them through your mistakes and you still failing them as a parent because you are coddling them so they won't fall into the trap that you didn't see coming as you grow up and you try to live Vicariously through your children because you are still quit young yourself mommy guilt is another stronghold that is very common but unrecognizable and never talked about just as well as daddy guilt when you say you don't want to do what your dad has done and you stride to do better but you are following the same pattern as your father and no matter how hard you try it seems like the way the system is in the world today we as a parent was meant to fail .But is that really true this world is a big test and once we trust in God we are able to change the cycle once we are obedient to what he instructed us to do.
"Thou shalt not bow down thyself to them, nor serve them: for I the Lord thy God am a jealous God, visiting the iniquity of the fathers upon the children unto the third and fourth generation of them that hate me;"
Exodus 20:5 KJV

Phase: 1. Our children become rebellious.
Phase: 2. The children become disrespectful.
Phase: 3. The children start picking up your old habitual habits.
Phase: 4. The children become numb to your feeling and tune out
everything you are teaching them it called selective hearing.
Phase: 5. You see yourself in your children and it becomes too late because they are all in too deep and they are too afraid to come to you because they don't want to face the truth and neither do you because you wish you could have tried harder to save them from what you were trying to protect them from.
Phase: 6. Now you come to the point that you want to help them through
this problem and you don't know where to begin.
Phase: 7. Now you looking to where you should have looked in the beginning and now you are praying to god for help when that was the first thing we should have done in the beginning when we saw the first sign we must cast our fears worries upon his throne and ask for forgiveness and repent daily to receive his mercy favor. And a spiritual breakthrough.
Phase: 8. New Beginning and I leave you with this.
"And he said unto them, Set your hearts unto all the words which I testify among you this day, which ye shall command your children to observe to do, all the words of this law."
Deuteronomy 32:46 KJV

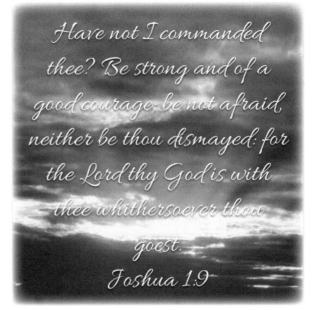

Proverbs 2:8 KJV; He keepeth the paths of judgment, and preserveth the way of his saints.

Joshua 1:9 KJV; Have not I commanded thee? Be strong and of a good courage; be not afraid, neither be thou dismayed: for the Lord thy God is with thee whithersoever thou goest.

DO YOU KNOW YOURSELF

What do you know about yourself
What make you happy
What can you bring to the table for yourself
Are you ambitious
Can you motivate yourself when you are down
Do you have will power to not subject yourself that can get you to become an addiction
Do you have a low self- esteem
Do you have a high-esteem
And you Confident
Do you have self-control
Are you happy with yourself
Do you love yourself
How do you know
Can you look in the Mirror and feel confident with in yourself
Can you see yourself cry in the mirror
Do feel you have to cover yourself up because you don't feel pretty or handsome enough
What makes you happy
Do you understand what is happiness is
Are you able to make yourself happy
Do you know how to self-motivated
Do you take responsibility of your own actions
Can you except your faults.

SEASONED MAN

What some women would call a seasonal man. Some men love women all types. Big, small, tall, and thin, then you have men who only know you from the back and then there is the other men who don't care what you look like as long as he can have his cake and eat it too, then comes in that seasonal man that is the moan who would like a big fat or ugly chick wine and dine her from September to the end of February, then he dumps her for March through August. That is the one who suppose to be the dime peace, in all reality, that is the gold-digger. Women beware of those seasonal guys who will promise the world to you and when the season ends, they cannot even remember your name.

SEASONED WOMAN

I am a very seasoned woman, too much of me might give you hypertension. I am a very seasoned woman, I am super sweet and will give you tasty treats savory in every way but would never complain every pound of me is worth more than euros. For what you are at the end of your storm you survived all the rest and obstacles and you have blessed many people with you kind words and unconditional loyalty and eternal love GOD has filled your bank account he is preparing your new home you are standing stronger you have earned a few more vertebrae disc in your spine that can't be destroyed and let's not forget you are a heiress of the king and the blood of Jesus flows through your vain so every tear you drop let be not for sorrow but for joy.

THE SECRET GARDEN

The secret garden of diligence an alluring inner being of resurrected life that brings the nuclear of your blessings as if it was an atomic bomb that killed every toxin in your unsaved soul bring fourth the new and take out the filth of my unsaved soul and let it blossom as the most rarest flower in the kingdom of our SAVIOR.

TURNING POINT

How many turning points in your life do you have to have to reach your destiny. Everyday something new happens to you and it seems strange, but rightly so. How do you go by excepting the new and turning down the old? Are you ready for change or is it that change can be ready for you? Life throw many optical your way that bring you to that turning point that you tried to ignore. Then ask yourself Am I ready for change or is change ready for me, here's where it gets interesting because once I reach the turning point in my life, I will be blunt but sincere. My head will be lifted up high and walk with a new-found respect when you reach your destiny, accept it with open arms.

GOD SPEAKS

With a whisper in your ear and the smell of your sweet essence and the beautiful glow of your bronze skin that is just as smooth and fine as silk when you talk, you put my body in a calm bus sensual mediation. Oh my GOD, my Jehovah my King, you have taken me where no man could ever take me. You have taught me things that people today are still trying to grasp. My King, I ask you can you whisper my next journey, so I can be you one of your messengers.

SMOKING MIRRORS

Are you in a recession, take that as a blessing to protect your assets, upgrade you will for life without strife. Humble yourself but never let your guard down. Don't frown, keep your smile, hold your head up because you are never alone. Take a sip of JESUS spiritually, and kick back and relax. GOD has protected the things that you have asked for, HE is watching you do the everyday foot work, don't think you are doing things in vain, your pain is victorious. Just know HE will love you, let's take a look at those Smokin Mirrors and see who is looking back at you.

John 11:25 KJV; Jesus said unto her, I am the resurrection, and the life: he that believeth in me, though he were dead, yet shall he live:

John 11:25-26 KJV; Jesus said unto her, I am the resurrection, and the life: he that believeth in me, though he were dead, yet shall he live: And whosoever liveth and believeth in me shall never dies. Believest thou this?

Psalms 143:10 KJV; Teach me to do thy will; for thou art my God: thy spirit is good; lead me into the land of uprightness.

Philippians 1:6 KJV; Being confident of this very thing, that he which hath begun a good work in you will perform it until the day of Jesus Christ:

1 Corinthians 13:13 KJV; And now abideth faith, hope, charity,
these three; but the greatest of these is charity.

STOP

This message is for my sisters and brothers that know the Lord and Savior Jesus Christ. Here are some rules to live by: Forgive but don't forget, if you believe go full force with your spirit and do not give into temptation. Love all, even thy enemies. Write your own personal love letters to the Lord and the victory over every situation in your life. Never settle for less and always expect great things and you shall receive them.

UNTITLED

Thru the wisdom and charisma in you, you are no longer the ugly duckling but a beautiful swan. Man may see you as a failure but to GOD you will always be a phenomenal achiever. As HIS vessel, speak the message HE has placed within you and watch as your words become real life blessings. Blessings not only for you but so that others can live free spiritually as if they were still in their Mother's wound. Than thank God for your phenomenal achievements, be blessed live strong and free! With your embrace give me a little taste of the nectar that flows through your veins and anointing me with your divine power of life that brings forth inner strength. Take away my baggage that is making me weak so that I can reach a new high like ganja in its purest form. Give me that nectar that flows through your veins and anoint me with your divine power, let me be fruitful from your nectar my Jehovah, let it runneth over me.

BROKEN BUT NOT DEFEATED

Thief in the night, wined and dined me but you were like a vampire in angel's clothing. I invited you into my home, but you tried to rape me spiritually and drain me financially. I was blind, I was weak, and I was broken but little did you know that I have the blood of the King of all angels in my life. HE shielded me and protected me from an un-angel like you, but my King told me what weapons formed against me will not prosper, I was broken but not defeated. Grab your weapon and fight with all your might and do not be blinded by a blood sucking un-angel, protect yourself and guard your throne so you will not be broken or defeated.

LOST AND WANT TO BE FOUND

I am child that cannot scream, I am a mute. I am bird that cannot tweet.
I am a soul that cannot rest.
I am blind and ca not see.
I am deaf and cannot hear.
I am trembling with regret and do not know how to vent.
I laugh but cannot be happy, I hurt with so much joy and sadness and so much fear. Then I look up and see, a man standing just a little further from me and his situation looks worse than me. So I smile and feel happy and took my shades off so I can see and take the ear plugs out of my ears that I may hear the sounds I could not hear. My soul can rest because I am at peace with me. My God has me spiritually, he teaches me and humbles me through His blessings that empowers me to get up and do it all over again. I am free, I can sing, and I am loved and not just me, but you too. Let's be that seed that grows into a beautiful flower because it was nurtured.

NECTAR

With your embrace give me a little taste of the nectar that flows through your veins and anoint me with your divine power of life that brings forth inner strength. Take away my baggage that is making me weak so that I can reach a new high like ganja in its purest form. Give me that nectar that flows through your veins and anoint me with your divine power, let me be fruitful from your nectar my Jehovah Jireh, let it runneth over me.

BE WITH ME

Be with me when I am all alone.
Be with me when I am confused.
Be with me when my head hits the pillow.
Be with me when I awake and take my first breathe.
Be with me because I never want to be alone.
Without you in my presence and in my heart I will be lost. You are my strength, my yellow brick road to freedom. When I am struggling, and the air feels so thin that I cannot breathe, I need you there, you are the fresh air that is why agape is always needed. So Lord, I ask you please be with me so I can stand tall and hold my head up high, that I may wear your shield of protection and love. Let me be your soldier in this war of greed, betrayal and deception, so Lord I ask you please be with me.

WARRIOR

I am a warrior for GOD, HE is the protector and I am HIS soldier that is ready for spiritual warfare. I am here to protect the souls and spirits of babies, fools, and the confused. I feed them knowledge, steer them in the right direction. I am a warrior for GOD. You all are welcomed to join the army with no consequences and received everlasting life, and to be able to free with no strings attached. To become a warrior, you must understand and know the LORD will protect you from the blood shatter and back stabbing. The LORD will be there trough all adversity. When the people you thought would have your back, are the same people kicking your back in. These people can be family, your friends, and coworker. Sometimes you have to step back and review the situation you are currently in, just know you are a warrior for GOD, use your shield and wear your armor to fulfill your destiny for what lies ahead for you. Know you are not the only one at war. Be ready to face the good, bad, and evil. Don't forget to use your weapon that way it was intended to be used or it will not serve the purpose it was intended for Are you ready for war? If you're not ready get ready for war is imminent. I am a soldier ready for GOD's war what about you?

DIVERSITY

Integration, segregation, love our nation. Peace for the LORD who is agape HE is our nation of integration and segregation. If we all live in agape of the LORD, we will be united by our race, culture, and religion, which is important to oneself. Love is everlasting, love that never ends no matter what creed, color, race, or religion you are. Live it love it, kill the worldly in you and find the spirit in you. It's a beautiful once you get to know our LORD and savior for yourself, then you will understand. Be blessed, live long and strong in the LORD.

ABANDONMENT OF A LOST SOUL

I have been abandoned, lost, and confused. I have been taken for granted. I am mentally, physically, financially, and spiritually in pain. This pain is unbearable. I am running in circles. I cross the street. I am walking to a dead end. I am hungry or LORD and lost. I am thirst or LORD. I am in a drought. Did you deal me the wrong hand in the game of life or am I playing the game correctly? I am hungry LORD for your wisdom. I am thirsting for you words. I have been abandoned. I am lost and confused, keep hitting brick walls and going in circles. Am I not hearing you right or is it that I am not listening. Have my quest ended because of my negligence or did you give up on me, or did I give up on you. Help me LORD help me. Help me see beyond what my eyes can see. I am lost and confused. I have abandoned you. You did not abandon me. I am hungry for your wisdom, I am thirsty for your words, I am a lost soul seeking your help LORD. Help me be free from all this anxiety.

Romans 8:28 KJV; And we know that all things work together for good to them that love God, to them who are the called according to his purpose.

I AM YOU & YOU ARE ME

I am ambitious.
I am free.
I am rambunctious.
I am cautious.
I am true.
I am you, you are me. We live vigorously. I ask the almighty to free us from the hater in our life and bring them to prosperity and don't bring them strife. I am you, you are me lets be free as free as the wind blows thru our hair and beneath our feet. I am cautious why? Because I am strong, and I will not let these haters take my all. You are you and I am me.

EXPLOSIVE

Explosive raging hormones like a volcano exploding at its highest denomination. I am explicit I am confused. However, the world is mine, is it ready for me or am I ready for the world. I am the highest denomination exploding with confidence and still standing my ground. I am the explicit inner child. I am exploding with rage that is blocking my thought and my blessings. Help me help you so you can understand me, and I can guide you.

MAP OF FORGIVENESS

Your past is the map to review the lesson you learn so you can't bring it to the present or your future therefore ending up going backwards. Stay steadfast and stay focused, its to learn from once you forgive yourself and others that taught you a valuable lesson revisiting will not hinder or effect you at all.

NURTURING MY HARVEST

1. When someone show me an eclectic cultural diverse spiritual life it's like enjoying the sweet supple taste that hits your pallet with great exquisite desire of an articulate conversation with a GOD Fearing Spiritual being.
When a person can feed you intellectually in such a succulent way
and can catch your attention by just the words, can have you hanging on every symbolic
symbol that has versatile acronyms that will have you thirsting for conversation about
the love of GOD with every living verse in the book that can save you from the rapture
and can set you free to receive eternal life and free you from all strongholds.
who am I but a spec one of many of GOD's children,
but the way the blood of CHRIST runs through my veins and the royalty
that make me an heir or a as long as I stay faithful,
my harvest will always be fruitful, as long as I keep my Harvest nurtured by
standing in the word of GOD, I will always have peace and Prosperity.

ONEMAN

I'm one-man the struggling nurturer. I strike with a blow that man can't begin to understand they only see the outer me. I am one-man. I strengthen me I strengthen you. I am willing to complete you if you let me lead, I can carry you on my back, and can be as sweet as honey because I am as strong as an ox. I mentally strengthen you with my work and encourage you with the holy spirit that is within me. I am one-man, I carry you with children like ankle weights thru the streets sometimes I can barely breath. I am unforgettable it seems. But easy to ignore like carrying you over hurdles that seem too hard to past, but if you listen to that inner voice it will guide you through every task. I am one-man, I have a test-i-mony. I am a one-woman-man that can bare the unbearable. I am a ONE-WOMAN-MAN who concurs one hurdle at a time and this is my test-i-mony.

DEAR GOD!!

Let us Bow our heads...Dear GOD, I come to you as humbly as I know how. I confess my sins, those known, and unknown. LORD you know I am not perfect, and I fall short every day of my life, but I want to take time out to say thank you for your grace, mercy, and favor. Thank you for my health, my family, my friends, the roof over my head, food on my table, all things. These things I have spoken unto you, that which is in me may have peace in the world, you may have tribulations, but be of good cheer, I have overcome the world!!!!

MONOLOGUE

My blueprint to a PHRESH START

A PHRESH START that sewed a seed to a new beginning.

OBJECTIVE: Development of total transparent reality-based program will recruit victims of domestic violence. All forms of child abuse as well as drug dependency for men as well as women.

DOMESIC VIOLENCE CHILD MELESTATION AND REHABILITATION:

PHASE ONE: Appropriate music to enhance the concept of the variety situations that are of concern for the victims.

PHASE TWO: Volunteers to read poetry, praise dancing, singing and prayer warriors.

PHASE THREE: Scrolling pictures of visitors to the EMOWERMENT PROGRAM (photo taken at entrance and added to projector to scroll).

PHASE FOUR: Actors to portray monologue for similarity between abuse and neglected families to abused and neglected plants from seedlings to maturity.

PHASE FIVE: Public would be allowed to speak out for those who want to start the healing process, which would inspire victims to begin rehabilitation.

PHASE SIX: Acquire sponsors.

PHASE SEVEN: Donations and gift bags for victim as well as resources.

PHASE EIGHT: Obtaining victim resources i.e. shelters, phone numbers, pantries, health providers, etc.

PHASE NINE: Obtain venues.

PHASE TEN: PHRESH START…. Turning victims victorious A NEW BEGINNING!

IMPLEMENTATIONS

- DJ to play selected music.
- Volunteers for poetry reading miming included (20 minutes).
- Singers (5-10 minutes)
- Actors for SHRINKING VIOLET monologue miming included (from seedling to mature plant) (25-30 minutes).
- Refreshments (30 minutes).
- Praise Dancers (5-10 minutes).
- Prayer Warriors (5-10 minutes).
- Photographer as people enter.
- Public Testimonials speak up to (20 minutes).
- Representative from the Empowerment Panel (15-20 minutes).
- Locating sponsors.
- Donations/Gift Bags for victims
- Obtaining Victim Resources
- Obtaining Venues
- Support Groups.
- Turning Victorious A NEW BEGINNING…….!

SELECTED SONGS TO BE PLAYED THRU-OUT THE PROGRAM

1) KIRK FRANKLIN – I Want to Be Happy
2) SHIRLEY MURDOCK – Love Me Better Than That
3) MICHELLE'LE – I'm So Glad I'm Standing Here Today
4) TASHA COBB – Break Every Chain
5) MARY MARY – I Am Walking
6) JAMES FORTUNE and FIYA – I Believe
7) TYRESE – Shame
8) TAMALA MANN – Take Me to The KING
9) YOLANDA ADAMS – Fragile Heart
10) YOLANDA ADAMS – Victory
11) YOLANDA ADAMS featuring DONNIE MC CLURKIN – The Prayer
12) KIRK FRANKLIN – I Smile
13) ZACARDI CORTEZ – GOD held me together
14) CHARLES JENKINS/FELLOWSHIP CHICAGO – War
15) BEBE & CECE WINANS – I'll Take You There
16) BISHOP PAUL S. MORTON – I'm Still Standing
17) CECE WINANS – Alabaster Box
18) DEON KIPPING – I Don't Look Like (What I've Been Through)
19) VICKIE YONI – Because Of Who You Are

DOMESTIC VIOLENCE

Victims of Domestic Violence need more immediate resources available to then. In my case, I was unaware to most of the services provided for victims of Domestic Violence. I may have been a typical victim who was cut-off from the rest of the world while having to protect my children as well. I had to run for my life to another state. In cases like this, you don't have a phone and every move you make is watched, so you do what you must do to try and survive until you can escape. This program is personal for me and What I promise to do if I were ever able to escape alive with my children. Victims in my situation are cut-off from the world and can't reach the resources thru normal channels. In the real world, you've been physically beaten, threatened and tormented and are afraid to ask for help. The lucky ones usually find help by the grace of GOD and can find someone to assist like a school counselor or someone passing and recognize the symptoms of Domestic Violence. Ask yourself a question…. if I am not allowed to use a phone or any communication devices as well as leave my home, how am I going to get help? This is where you must be creative. We can try sending HELP forms home from school with our children that will be signed, dated, and returned. In this case some abusers are not paying attention and you may be able to reach out, this way the school is fir first cry out source for abused children. The only thing the school is responsible for is forwarding the information to the correct resources, which, means all forms returned will be forwarded to the resource outreach facilitator. There are a lot of people who are not comfortable having their personal lives on display (especially victims) for all to see and judge. Privacy is deserved, needed, and expected. Remember victims are afraid their abuser will find out they were reaching out for help, which, could keep them from getting the help this is greatly needed before something devastating happens!

CHILD MOLESTATION ABUSE

Often in homes with Domestic Abuse you will find CIILD MOLESTATION. It begins with an absent dad/mom (regardless the reason) and what dad/mom thought would be a great father/mother figure for the absentee parent to their child and they turn out to be a molester/abuser.

It begins with you noticing Mr./Ms. Molester starting to help the child more than the other children and more than usual, in addition, Mr./Ms. Molester starts buying special gifts, giving money, spending more "quality time" most of it without your knowledge. This goes on for a while until you no longer know this child you gave birth to. Your child is no longer doing well in school and starts pulling away from family and friend and only wants time and attention from Mr./Ms. Molester to assist and help them with their problems. Remember the child sees Mr./Ms. Molester abuse you as well and your child's respect for you is now a problem.

Mr./Ms. Molester has your child doing things sexually no adult would ever think of while keeping it a secret from you. The molested child needs mental and physical help as well to ensure them absolutely none of what has happened to them is their fault.

Meanwhile, Mr./Ms. Molester is now Mr./Ms. Child Abuser and commences to abuse/neglect the other children as well if Mr./Ms. Child Abuser is no molesting them. The children are neglected food and proper clothing while Mr./Ms. Molester wears the latest outfits and footwear, in addition, the rest of the children are severely punished for the smallest infractions for not following the rules I.e. spanked with belt buckles in the face, then kept home from school the next day so authorities will not find out. Telling them if anyone asks, tell them it was a mistake by the other parent.

If the custodial parent can't help themselves how ae they supposed to get their children help?

Again, the school is the first defense. Teachers, counselors, social workers, and school nurses should be re-educated on seeing the signs of abuse. No! This is no easy task, but the best chance abused children have.

AS a village, let's get involved!!! See something say something. We understand these children are not always upfront with this information since they were told the punishment will be severe for not following the rules. Also remember Mr./Ms. Abuser needs to always maintain complete control over everything and everyone to keep their secret from getting out so the abuse can continue. and they have no worries of authorities intervening.

After receiving the HELP form and it has been forwarded to the proper outreach facility, the outreach facilitator them follows up with the custodial parent, teacher, counselor, social worker, and nurse before closing the case as unwarranted. There can be simple ways put in place for victims to notify authorities of abuse i.e. special way the parent signs the paperwork.

DRUG/ALCOHOL ABUSE

People who are controlled by drug and/or alcohol abuse will also benefit from this program. Resources will be made available to both men/women who suffer from this disease. Everyone is welcomed, and privacy is expected. Their needs will be evaluated by professionals for them to receive the best care and continue the road to recovery.

The time the drug/alcohol abuser must spend time in an in-patient or outpatient rehabilitation facility is based on the licensed professional recommendations.

Families are welcomed to attend for the drug/alcohol abuser to fully recover from this disease. Families should be part of the recovery process when possible. No one can do it alone!!

REHABILITATION

Rehabilitation is the final step to becoming whole and sage again. This includes mental, psychological, emotional, and physical therapy for the families. Everyone must complete all visits to all doctors who will be working together for one cause. To ensure the injured no longer must suffer in silence and now have a voice which was once stolen/silent.

MONOLOGUE

She/he begins to complain about dinner and the noise the children are making while playing. Mr./Ms. Abuser starts yelling at mom/dad to cook something else and keep the children quiet.

At this point chaos begins. They begin to throw things at mom/dad swearing them the whole time. Nothing is good enough. Mr./Ms. Abuser starts to bring up the same old issues swearing the whole time and complaining why everything is mom/dad's fault.

The children as well now are familiar with the signs when Mr./Ms. Abuser are on the war path and begins to get nervous as well. Scurrying to bed to avoid the abuse.

Suddenly, you hear an OOF!! It's Mr./Ms. Abuser hitting mom/dad with something. Then repeatedly until mom/dad cries out loud.

The seedling started to grow and was looking beautiful until mom/dad had to go to the hospital due to the beating. It was so awful mom/dad needed stitches and a cast. The seedling plant wasn't nourished so it didn't flourish.

A few days later mom/dad watered the plant and noticed there was no food in the house and they needed to buy food to feed the family and Mr./Ms. Abuser come home early and noticed mom/dad wasn't there and waited until mom/dad returned to start the abuse again because they did not follow the rules. The children seen how vicious Mr./Ms. Abuser began plummeting them as well. Now mom/dad and one the children needed to be rushed to the hospital.

Once their mom/dad finally realized this can't continue, mom/dad noticed finally the children were being harmed because this time they didn't do enough to protect them.

When the authorities asked the child what happened, the child replied I fell. When the authorities asked the mom/dad what happened, mom/dad began to tell everything not withholding anything about their abuse as well as the child abuse.

The police arrested Mr./Ms. Abuser and they were no longer allowed in the home as well as restraining order placed to keep the family safe. The plant them received the water, food and nourishment needed and began to bloom the most beautiful flower mom/dad had ever seen.

CLOSING MONOLOGUE

As the monologue is going on the stage there will be a funeral with the eulogy and as the lights come on there will be a marriage with someone to JESUS CHRIST. There will be angels descending from the ceiling and Prayer Warriors will be sitting with and among all the actors on stage.

Praise dancers dancing around the room. The lights go off during the final prayer and the Prayer and Dance Warriors begin praying for everyone in the room. Towards the end of the prayer, the lights come back up for everyone to enjoy and participate in the ending of the prayer.

Wherefore he is able also to save them to the uttermost that come unto God by him, seeing he ever liveth to make intercession for them.
Hebrews 7:25

And we know that all things work together for good to them that love God, to them who are the called according to his purpose.
Romans 8:28

And we know that all things work together for good to them that love God, to them who are the called according to his purpose.
Romans 8:28

And now abideth faith, hope, charity, these three; but the greatest of these is charity.
1 Corinthians 13:13

Therefore if any man be in Christ, he is a new creature: old things are passed away; behold, all things are become new.
2 Corinthians 5:17

Have not I commanded thee? Be strong and of a good courage; be not afraid, neither be thou dismayed: for the Lord thy God is with thee whithersoever thou goest.
Joshua 1:9

He keepeth the paths of judgment, and preserveth the way of his saints.
Proverbs 2:8

Jesus said unto her, I am the resurrection, and the life: he that believeth in me, though he were dead, yet shall he live: And whosoever liveth and believeth in me shall never die. Believest thou this?
John 11:25-26

Jesus said unto her, I am the resurrection, and the life: he that believeth in me, though he were dead, yet shall he live: And whosoever liveth and believeth in me shall never die. Believest thou this?
John 11:25-26

Being confident of this very thing, that he which hath begun a good work in you will perform it until the day of Jesus Christ.
Philippians 1:6

Teach me to do thy will; for thou art my God: thy spirit is good; lead me into the land of uprightness.
Psalms 143:10

And now abideth faith, hope, charity, these three; but the greatest of these is charity.
1 Corinthians 13:13

And we know that all things work together for good to them that love God, to them who are the called according to his purpose.
Romans 8:28

For bodily exercise profiteth little: but godliness is profitable unto all things, having promise of the life that now is, and of that which is to come.
1 Timothy 4:8 KJV

Printed in the United States
By Bookmasters